How to Make Money Online

A Proven Step-by-Step Guide and List of the Top Twenty Online Resources To Make $1000s a Month

Introduction

Making money is now more important than ever due to the unstable and unpredictable economic situation that plagues us. Today, income is not only generated with one regular job, people are now starting to look for alternative sources of income.

The intersection of business and technology makes it possible for an average person to still work on a standard 8 hour job while earning money on the side. This is where money-making online tools become a necessary part of your quest for financial freedom.

This book will share with you the many platforms available online that can provide you with an opportunity to sell products or services. This guide is divided into 2 parts, part 1 is for selling goods and the top 10 online platforms to sell general merchandise like on ebay and Amazon to specifc and niche goods such as Fotolalia, Kindle and Blogs. Part 2 is all about selling services, such as accounting, bookkeeping, graphic designing or writing for professional services and simple tasks such as watching videos, playing games or just clicking a link for niche services.

Each platform will discuss:

What can be sold?
Setting up an account overview

Monthly seller fees
Possible income levels
Time Requirement
Pros & Cons
Examples
A getting started Checklist
FAQ & Best Practices

With these online resources, you can retake control of your finances. You can earn thousands at the comfort of your home. Become a profitable master at online selling!

Introduction

Part One: Make Money Online Selling Goods

Chapter One: General Merchandise & Platforms
1. eBay
2. Craigslist
3. Etsy
4. Amazon
5. Own Online Store

Chapter Two: Specific or Niche Merchandise & Platforms
6. Stock Photos Using iStockphoto, Shutterstock & Fotolia
7. Apps & Music Using iTunes & Android
8. Articles & Blogs Using Flippa
9. eBooks Using Kindle
10. Game Accounts & Items Using World of Warcraft

Part Two: Make Money Online Selling Services

Chapter Three: Professional Services & Platforms
1. odesk
2. elance
3. Fiverr
4. Zaarly
5. Freelancer

Chapter Four: Specific or Niche Services & Platforms
6. Surveys Using Globaltestmarket & Crowdology
7. Affiliate marketing Using Amazon Associates & Personal Blogs
8. Pay per Click Using Swagbucks
9. Write Reviews & Feedback Using Slicethepie
10. Crowdfunding Using Kickstarter, Indiegogo & Gofundme

Conclusion

Each section includes:
What can be sold?
Setting up an account overview
Monthly seller fees
Possible income levels
Time Requirement
Pros & Cons
Examples
A getting started Checklist
FAQ & Best Practices

Part One: Make Money Online Selling Goods

Selling goods and products online have never been easier and more profitable. The advantages online stores offer have made it very lucrative and more preferable compared to traditional brick and mortar stores. Most entrepreneurs, especially beginners, are attracted to the savings and efficiency that is made possible by e-commerce.

Traditional stores require significant investment, such as upfront expenses, indoor furnishing and equipment that entails recurring costs, such as utilities, payroll and maintenance. These stores have also limited reach, often only covering the community where it is located.

On the other hand, online stores can write off expenses normally associated with traditional stores. You do not have to pay for electricity, water, rent, staff and upkeep. Once you take your store online, virtually everybody who has access to the Internet around the world can access and purchase your goods.

Various online platforms have taken advantage of the e-commerce phenomenon by providing sellers a virtual venue to set up shop. The most popular platforms are discussed in the succeeding two chapters. To help you decide which platform you will choose, each section will have a discussion on:

What can be sold?
Setting up an account overview
Monthly seller fees
Possible income levels
Time Requirement
Pros & Cons
Examples
A getting started Checklist
FAQ

Chapter 1 presents the top 5 platforms that you can choose that is open for almost all kinds of goods that is sold. Chapter 2 presents another set of 5 platforms that are well known for selling specific or niche types of goods.

Chapter 1: General Merchandise & Platforms

EBay

What can be sold?

1. Antiques; such as books, manuscripts, ethnographic items and decorative arts
2. Books; such as collectibles, audio books, catalogs, fiction, literature, magazine back issues, textbooks and non-fiction books
3. Clothing, Shoes & Fashion Accessories; such as women, men and kid's fashion, handbags, jewelry, watches and beauty products
4. Collectibles; such as autographs, bottles, clocks, metal wares, paper, pens and writing instruments, postcards, rocks, memorabilia, stamps, coin and paper money, vintage and tools
5. Electronics; such as computers, servers, monitors, printers, software, manuals, cameras, laptops, tablets and smart phones
6. Entertainment; such as video games, consoles, music, video, movies and tickets
7. Home and garden; such as yard and garden tools, crafts, home improvement, furniture, mattresses, housekeeping and maintenance, repairs and pet supplies
8. Motor; such as cars, trucks, motorcycles, parts and accessories, tools, supplies and merchandise
9. Sports; such as cycling, fishing, fitness, golf, hunting, indoor and outdoor games, tennis, water and water sports-related products
10. Toys; such as action figures, building toys, classic toys, costumes, educational, electronic, games, marbles, trading cards, stuff animals and wholesale toys
11. Real estate; such as commercial, land, manufactured homes and residential

12. Travel; such as tickets, car rentals, cruises, lodging, luggage, maps, travel accessories and vacation packages
13. Others; such as adult-exclusive, funeral and cemetery arrangements, security, religious supplies and even niche categories

Setting up an account overview

EBay requires advanced registration. Registering as an individual seller is very easy; it only requires your name, email and a password. However, if you plan to register as a business, you need your business name, address, business contact person, and primary contact numbers. EBay will call or text you to give verification PIN to confirm your eBay seller account.

Monthly seller fees

Subscription fees are charged depending on your store type and terms of payment:

1. Basic $19.95 per month or $15.95 per month when 1 year is paid in advance
2. Premium $59.95 per month or $49.95 per month when paid in advance
3. Anchor $199.95 per month or $179.95 per month when paid in advance

Every time you list an item, you are charged an insertion fee, regardless of the quantity you are selling. Free subscriptions give you 150 free insertion fee listings per month 500 for the premium and 2,500 for the anchor store. Insertion fees differ per category but the range is around $0.30. A final value fee is also charged when you are able to sell a product. It is calculated as the 10% amount of the selling cost plus the shipping. Payments of these fees can be automatically set up using your PayPal, debit or credit card.

Possible income levels

Depending on your product, income levels vary. However, eBay reports that their top seller to date has over $152,000 in sales in one month alone by selling business and industrial products. A seller of phones and accessories has revenue of $66,000 in one month. Clothing, shoes and accessories seller generated $43,000 in one month.

Time Requirement

This platform only requires 1 to 2 hours in total a day to check for status of sales or orders. Peaks are experienced when there are holidays, customer complaints or returns.

Currently eBay offers a Valet Service that will do everything you for you. From listing to selling to even shipping. However, eBay charges 30% commission for every sale made by their Valets.

Pros & Cons

Pros

1. User friendly, great for beginner sellers
2. Requires no money to start
3. Allows wide range of products and lenient on sellers

Cons

1. Listing fees charged regardless of sale
2. Less affluent pool of buyers
3. Risk for non payment

Examples

Fashion accessory
Kitchen knife
Stuffed toy

A getting started Checklist

1. Your product
2. At least 4 photos
3. Listing
4. Preference between Auction or Fixed Price
5. PayPal account
6. Valid credit or debit card or other bank account information
7. Payment methods that you accept

FAQ & Best Practices

Consider auction-based selling for rare, one of a kind and niche items. Use the buy now option for products that have competition from other sellers.

Craigslist

What can be sold?

1. Antiques
2. Appliances
3. Beauty products
4. Books
5. Cars
6. Phones
7. Computers
8. Furniture
9. Jewelry
10. Tools
11. Video games

It is also a portal for personal and topic-based discussion, services, jobs and gigs.

Setting up an account overview

This platform only requires basic registration. Craigslist only requires your email account to set up a user account.

Monthly seller fees

Craigslist offer free posting, except for specific locations, which have charges from $5 to $75 depending on the category of the advertisement.

Visit craigslist to have more detailed information on the cost of posting an ad based on your location.

Possible income levels

Depending on the products sold, users report from $200 a day to $8000 a month.

Time Requirement

Posting an ad can be done within 5 minutes. Shipping a product will only require your coordination for at most 30 minutes. You can use this platform on your free time.

Pros & Cons

Pros

1. User friendly
2. Anonymity
3. No middlemen, fees or commissions

Cons

1. Not as reputable as eBay and Amazon
2. Known for controversies and bartering
3. Limited reach and based only on your location

Examples

Appliances
House materials
Garage sales

A getting started Checklist

1. Locality
2. Post title, price and posting description
3. Pictures

FAQ & Best Practices

Avoid spamming ads as this may only cause account suspension. Instead spread out ads throughout the day. Do not be tempted to post the same ads on different areas. Choose the area you think has the most chances for success.

Etsy

What can be sold?

Note that Etsy sells only either vintage or handmade products. Product categories include:

1. Art
2. Home & living
3. Mobile accessories
4. Jewelry
5. Vintage
6. Craft supplies
7. Fashion for men, women and kids
8. Toys and knick-knacks

Items require at least 20 years of age to be eligible as a vintage product.

Setting up an account overview

Etsy requires your name, email address and a password to set up an account. Alternatively, it can use your Facebook account to fill in the details.

Monthly seller fees

1. Listing fee of $0.20 per item
2. Commission rate of 3.5% per sale

Possible income levels

Average monthly sales reported around $1000.

Time Requirement

Since Etsy requires selling only handcrafted items, it may require a significant amount of your time. Vintage items need to be properly searched and validated. Expect at least a month to amass a sizeable sales inventory.

Pros & Cons

Pros

1. Go-to website for customers looking for handmade and vintage products
2. User friendly
3. International reach

Cons

1. More sellers and more competition
2. Lack of peer support
3. Require significant promotion of your Etsy store and products

Examples

Kraft papers
Crochet patterns
Vintage dresses

A getting started Checklist

1. Eye-catching banner and design of your Etsy store
2. Unique shop name
3. Payment options

FAQ & Best Practices

Start handcrafting something that you feel passionate about in doing. Alternatively, Etsy has recently allowed mass produced products that have a handcrafted look to it, if you do not have time for making your own products, you can source them instead.

Amazon

What can be sold?

1. Books, textbooks, magazines and eBooks
2. Movies, videos, musical instruments, video and digital games
3. Cameras, photo and video equipment
4. Laptops, tablets, desktop computers and accessories
5. Fashion and beauty products
6. Grocery and gourmet food, wine, pantry and ingredients
7. Toys, birthdays and registries
8. Home, kitchen, dining, furniture, bed, bath, appliance, pet supplies, fixtures, tools and hardware
9. Sports, exercise, athletic clothing, team sports, fans shop, collectibles, cycling, action and gears
10. Automotive and industrial, cars, tires, wheels, motorcycle, janitorial and safety equipment
11. Digital media, music, apps, games, cloud drives and videos

Setting up an account overview

Amazon requires advanced registration. Amazon requires name, email address, password and legal name if registering as a business. You may also need to provide your tax identification numbers and bank account details.

Monthly seller fees

1. Listing fee of $.0.99 for free subscribers
2. Professional seller fee of $39.99 per month
3. Variable fees for Fulfilled by Amazon or FBA sellers

Possible income levels

Amazon sellers report figures for as low as $2.50 to as high as $100,000 per month.

Time Requirement

Amazon's time requirement is variable but relatively the same as eBay. However, Amazon offers Fulfillment by Amazon to relieve sellers from tedious work. Should you opt for the FBA system, you need only at most 1 hour total in a day to monitor your shop.

Pros & Cons

Pros

1. Greatest reach and most popular
2. Buyers have highest purchasing power
3. Credibility and trust

Cons

1. Need items in bulk to make profit
2. Commission fees of 15% to 25%
3. Stricter rules for sellers, photos and product listings

Examples

Abs toning belt
Steel watch
Electric razor

A getting started Checklist

1. A well-stocked inventory
2. Sourcing network
3. Boxes for shipping to FBA
4. Business plan for your Amazon store

FAQ & Best Practices

Amazon is ideally for experienced sellers, who have a lot of inventory in their stocks. Consider using an introductory price to generate sales and positive feedbacks. When your profile reaches the sales statistics you need to make a good impression to your potential customers, adjust the prices.

Own Online Store

What can be sold?

Since it is your own store, you have virtually full freedom on the list of products that you can sell. There will be no restrictions on what products you can sell or on what type of format you want them advertised.

Setting up an account overview

Not applicable.

Monthly seller fees

Not applicable. However, depending on the platform that you will use, either a simple blog which is free or a fully automated ecommerce website, you may need to pay certain costs. Ecommerce software will range from $15 to $1000 subscription fees.

Possible income levels

Variable, your earnings will depend on your products.

Time Requirement

The freedom offered by your own online store comes at a price. You will be in charge for publishing, adding content, maintaining the site and checking for bugs or errors. Most of the business processes, such as listing products, posting them, monitoring and coordinating payment and shipping sales will require time.

Pros & Cons

Pros

1. Virtually no monthly fees and minimal transaction fees, if you choose a free platform
2. Full control of brand, content, product and business identity
3. Freedom from feedback and controls

Cons

1. Upfront fees when using e-commerce software
2. Extremely time consuming
3. Requires advertisements to bring customers to your online store

Examples

Macbook decals
Electronics and gadgets store
Baby products

A getting started Checklist

1. Social media or blog account that can host the store
2. IT professional, who can help you set up
3. Ecommerce software if needed

FAQ & Best Practices

Use social media to advertise your online store to your network of friends. Provide incentives to those who share your post or updates so you can gain as much promotions as possible. Use your own store to try out the ecommerce business before committing to paid subscriptions from other platforms.

Chapter Two: Specific or Niche Merchandise & Platforms

Stock Photos Using iStockphoto, Shutterstock & Fotolia

What can be sold?

Photos are intellectual properties and they cannot be used or duplicated without permission. You receive sales in terms of royalties from photos that you lend using these platforms.

Categories for photos include:

1. Abstract
2. Animals and wildlife
3. Arts
4. Backgrounds and textures
5. Beauty and fashion
6. Buildings and landmarks
7. Food and drink
8. Icons
9. Interiors
10. Nature
11. Patterns
12. People
13. Vintage

Setting up an account overview

Basic registration, these platforms require only username, email and password. Register as a Contributor so you can have the platforms manage your portfolio.

Monthly seller fees

No registration fees. iStockphoto: Royalty fees from 15% to 45% per download of your photo. Shutterstock: $0.25 to $28 per download. Fotolia: Royalty fees from 20% to 63% per download.

Possible income levels

Levels average from $100 to $ 200 per month depending on the demand of your photo.

Time Requirement

All you have to do is take pictures, upload them on the platforms as a contributor. You can use your free time to take photos.

Pros & Cons

Pros

1. Legal backing of the platform
2. Local and foreign representation
3. Administrative support allowing you to focus on the art

Cons

1. Profit is cut because of commissions
2. No contact with clients
3. Competition

Examples

Wedding picture
Nature photo
Abstract patterns

A getting started Checklist

1. Photos in JPG format

2. At least 4.0 megapixels
3. Vectors maximum of 15mb
4. Illustrations at least 4.0 megapixels
5. Videos from 4 to 60 seconds

FAQ & Best Practices

Due to the competition, consider creating a brand of your own in your photos that will differentiate you from the rest of the photographers. You can also submit your current images and gain an idea on how the market receives them.

Apps & Music Using iTunes & Android

What can be sold?

1. Games
2. Education
3. Lifestyle
4. Health and fitness
5. Productivity
6. Sports
7. Business
8. Utilities
9. Finance
10. Medical
11. Navigation
12. Weather
13. Music

Setting up an account overview

Advanced registration is required, details such as name, address, email address, credit card or other payment methods will be needed and register as a Developer.

Monthly seller fees

$25-$99 per year and should you outsource the development of the app, costs vary from simple apps costing $1000 to the more complex games reaching $250,000.

Possible income levels

Income is variable and depending on the performance of your app. However, based on the average downloads per month per app; you can receive around $2000 to $21,000. The infamous Angry Birds app brought in $50 million due to advertising revenues.

Time Requirement

Time needed is dependent on the complexity of your app. Survey results show an average of 4 months to develop an app.

Pros & Cons

Pros

1. Almost worldwide customer base
2. Highly popular
3. Can double as an advertising platform

Cons

1. Competition with more than millions of developers
2. Large investment and upfront fees
3. Requires significant amount of technical knowledge

Examples

Family locator
Gas manager
Atlas

A getting started Checklist

1. Concept and target customer for the app
2. Xcode and other development software downloaded from either Apple or Google
3. Text editor, graphics and other programming software
4. iOS development tools can only run on Macs

FAQ & Best Practices

Consider publishing your app for free to generate feedbacks and number of download. When you reach the number of statistics that you want, you can host a variety of companies that can use your app to advertise their products.

Articles & Blogs Using Flippa

What can be sold?

Blogs are used as virtual advertising space, the more followers and networks with other blogs it has the more valuable it becomes. Once a blog has reached a large of amount of followers, it becomes a lucrative virtual space.

Setting up an account overview

These platforms only require basic registration such as a username and password. Blogs also require your customized blog address.

Monthly seller fees

1. Listing fee of $29
2. Commission fee of 5%
3. Blog software and hosting range from free to $299 per year

Possible income levels

Successful blogs can be flipped from $10,000 to $100,000 per blog.

Time Requirement

1 day to build the blog, complete with homepages, subsections and other content. Frequent updates such as new articles, photos and videos are needed to generate movement in your blog.

Pros & Cons

Pros

1. No monetary investment
2. Earn from doing something you feel passionate about
3. Large profit margin due to a bidding structure

Cons

1. Requires months to years to amass followers
2. A variety of skills are needed aside from the actual blog content. You need to be good at writing, photography and SEO.
3. You may find it difficult to part with something that you have invested a lot of your personal time in doing.

Examples

Domain name
Travel blog
Weapons blog

A getting started Checklist

1. Popular or niche topic
2. Advertisers and registered followers
3. Statistics or number of visitors
4. Screenshots

FAQ

You can always outsource some of the content of the blog; you can hire freelance writers for the articles or photographers for the images and videos. Your main task then is the management and promotion of the blog and.

eBooks Using Kindle

What can be sold?

EBooks are downloadable books that can be read by virtually all kinds of smart phones, tables and computers. You act as both author and seller of these eBooks.

Categories

1. Romance
2. Science fiction and fantasy
3. Children
4. Teen and young adult
5. Mystery, thriller and suspense
6. Literature and fiction
7. Erotica
8. Religion and spirituality
9. Business and money
10. Biographies and memoirs
11. Self-help guides

Setting up an account overview

Having an Amazon account automatically registers you to the Kindle Direct Publishing service.

Monthly seller fees

1. Commission fee of 15%
2. Royalty rates from 35% to 70%

Possible income levels

Self published books are sold at a minimum of $2.99 to $9.99. Authors report an average of $500- $1000 monthly revenues. Amanda Hocking, author of Fifty Shades of Grey, generated $2.5 million from self-publication alone.

Time Requirement

Self published eBooks range from 5,000 to 100,000 word contents. Depending on your speed of writing 5,000 words on the average take 2 to 4 days to write, format and package. Publishing in Amazon takes less than 5 minutes.

Pros & Cons

Pros

1. No need for an ISBN number
2. No monetary investment should you write yourself
3. No shipping charges to your customers

Cons

1. Requires excellent writing skills
2. Hundreds of competition from other authors
3. Very vulnerable to reader feedback

Examples

Horror book
Science fiction and fantasy book
Cook books

A getting started Checklist

1. Topic and target readers
2. Social media to advertise your publications
3. Download KindleGen, Previewer, Plugin and Kindle App
4. eBook cover

5. US sellers are required to provide their SSN for tax payment
6. Copyright page

FAQ

If writing is a skill that you feel not confident in doing then you can outsource the actual writing of the content to freelancers. You will pay a one-time fixed payment to the writer but all rights to the book will be yours by virtue of a ghostwriting agreement. You can also have someone design the eBook cover for you.

Game Accounts & Items Using World of Warcraft

What can be sold?

Virtual in-game items are the products for this online business. These are a variety of items that are used by online game players, who prefer a quick way to get hold of expensive or rare items without having to spend time playing their way through the game.

Categories:

1. Equipment, clothing, accessories and gear
2. Mounts or transportation
3. Ships, vehicles and avatars
4. In-game currency
5. Game accounts in their entirety

Setting up an account overview

Basic registration is required to installing and subscribing to the virtual game of your choice. You need a username, name, email address and birthday.

Monthly seller fees

1. Upfront payment for game $12- $15
2. Subscription for game $25 for two months

Possible income levels

10,000 in game gold are sold an average of $6. Gears, leveling and accounts sell from $100 to $1000+

Time Requirement

Intensive dedication is need for this endeavor. This requires complete commitment to the game, the more time spent, the more gold is earned and the higher the chances to get quality items to resell for real money. Average time to complete game requirements that will net you with the gold or items that you can sell may range from 1 to 3 months depending on the hours you spent a day.

Pros & Cons

Pros

1. Very satisfying if video games are your passion
2. High profit margins if you are lucky with random rewards
3. Easy to outsource to other willing players

Cons

1. Time-consuming
2. Market rates fluctuate
3. Game updates or changes, called patches, may change the economy of your chosen game.

Examples

Gold to dollars
World of Warcraft gold
Diablo 3 gold

A getting started Checklist

1. Choose best professions to generate gold, such as skinning, herbal collecting, mining and enchanting.
2. Run instances on Outlands or Northrend
3. Participate in boss fights and difficult missions
4. Processor, ram and video card that can run the game

FAQ & Best Practices

Although it may be tempting to choose a free online game to cut back on costs, most players of paid subscriptions games have more purchasing power. Choose games that are the most popular, such as World of Warcraft, Diablo and Final Fantasy.

Part Two: Make Money Online Services

Aside from goods or products, you can also sell services online. With the power of the Internet to connect professionals across the globe, clients who require your specific qualification or expertise can reach you.

There is an entire industry of service-based business in the web today. Engineers, writers, graphic artists and software programmers can provide professional services to a client in another location or even country. Other simple tasks such as clicking a link, watching a video, cleaning a house or completing a survey can also be exchanged for a price.

Due to the differences in foreign exchange rate of currencies, most clients take advantage of the relatively low labor cost that is charged by these professionals. On the other hand, freelancers are able to cash in on this income because of the high exchange rate on their own countries.

Making money online through freelancing gives you an opportunity to have an alternative source of income aside from your regular day job. You have flexible use of your time and you can also work on the comforts of your home.

Chapter Three: Professional Services & Platforms

Odesk

What can be sold?

Service categories include:

1. Web development
2. Software development
3. Networking and information systems
4. Writing and translation

5. Administrative support
6. Design and multimedia
7. Customer service
8. Sales and marketing
9. Business services

Setting up an account overview

This platform requires advanced registration. You will need to provide your name, email address, country and password. Odesk will require you to undergo several tests that are related to your chosen expertise. Writing will require grammar and vocabulary tests, administrative services will require filing, organizing and reading exams.

The more tests you take and the more complete your profile becomes, odesk will reward you with additional application quotas. Good feedback scores also add to your quota.

Monthly seller fees

1. No registration fees
2. Commission of 10%
3. Withdrawal fee of $1

Possible income levels

Average contract cost from $50 to $2,500 fixed price and $5-$140 per hour per contract. Depending on your speed and quality of delivery, you can receive average monthly earnings of $300-$500 inclusive of bonuses for job well done. Odesk reports up to $100,000 of salary paid per person.

Time Requirement

Flexible and dependent on your availability, you may opt to commit your full or part of your working time as a freelancer. 5,000 word articles take 2 to 4 days to write, administrative services 4 hours for per day and contracts for more than 3 to 6 months.

Pros & Cons

Pros

1. Flexible use of time
2. Strong support for hourly freelancers
3. High demand for outsourced services

Cons

1. Competition from other freelancers
2. Limited applications per month
3. Long clearing time for payments

Examples

Writing job
Web developer service
Virtual assistant

A getting started Checklist

1. Portfolio
2. Profile image
3. Bank or PayPal account to receive your earnings

FAQ & Best Practices

Take as many tests as you can, this will give you better chances to be chosen by potential clients. Also be very customer friendly to your clients as the numbers of applications for contracts you are given in a month are dependent on the feedback you receive from them.

Elance

What can be sold?

1. IT and programming
2. Design and multimedia
3. Writing and translation
4. Sales and marketing
5. Admin support
6. Engineering and manufacturing
7. Finance and management
8. Legal services

Setting up an account overview

Elance requires advanced registration. Aside from entering your name, email address and location or use your Facebook and LinkedIn account to create your elance profile, you need to add other fields. Your skills and areas of expertise need to be entered. Take note that whatever competency that you entered, elance will recommend you to take tests that are related to it.

Monthly seller fees

1. Basic subscription is free
2. Paid plans of $10, $20 and $60 per month
3. Additional connects to apply for contracts at $1 per connect
4. Commission fee of 8.75%

Possible income levels

Freelancers report an average of $200- $5,000 per month. Contract prices range from $50 to $2000.

Time Requirement

Flexible and dependent on your availability, freelancing relies on your choice of time to work. You may opt to commit your full or part of your working time as a freelancer. 5,000 word articles take 2 to 4 days to write, administrative services 4 hours for per day and contracts for more than 3 to 6 months.

Pros & Cons

Pros

1. Low rate of commissions from the platform
2. User-friendly
3. Option to spend more connects to prioritize your application over competition

Cons

1. Competition with other freelancers
2. Fake or spam contracts can trick you into using up your connects
3. Regular income is not guaranteed since it is dependent on clients offering jobs

Examples

App development
Marketing assistance
Translation services

A getting started Checklist

1. Profile picture
2. Portfolio
3. Verification from elance by submitting valid IDs

FAQ

Bid low to get contracts when starting, you will need to increase your number of clients and earnings to make your profile as impressive as possible. Alternatively, you can also outsource your own projects to others. By being a sort of employer, you can use your profile to get jobs and charge a small finder's fee when you hire others to do the work for you.

Fiverr

What can be sold?

1. Graphics and design
2. Online marketing
3. Writing and translations
4. Video and animation
5. Music and audio
6. Programming and technology
7. Bizarre jobs

Setting up an account overview

Fiverr only requires basic registration, such as name and email address to begin searching for jobs or gigs.

Monthly seller fees

1. Commission rate of 20%
2. Transfer fee of 2% or $1

Possible income levels

Gigs at $5- $500 with gig extras from additional $1 to $100 for rush or additional tasks.

Time Requirement

Fiverr tasks require a variety of timeframes. Some services can be done in under a minute while other require longer periods of time. As much as $100 per day can be earned when performing highly technical and urgent requests.

Pros & Cons

Pros

1. User friendly navigation
2. Supportive community
3. Relatively easy tasks to perform

Cons

1. One of the highest commission fees
2. 2 weeks clearing time
3. Jobs are automatically accepted, no chance to decline

Examples

Drawing jobs
SEO for Google
Sing a happy birthday song

A getting started Checklist

1. Profile
2. Portfolio
3. Tools for your chosen service

FAQ

Fiverr offers seller levels:

1. Level 1: active for 30 days at completed at least 10 orders
2. Level 2: Over 50 orders for the past 2 months
3. Top rated: determined by Fiverr editors based on seniority, sales, ratings, customer care and community leadership

Each level increases the amount of gigs that you can post and extras that you can add.

Zaarly

What can be sold?

1. Training
2. Tutorials
3. Errands
4. Chores
5. Cleaning
6. Gardening
7. Car care
8. Home organization
9. Personal services

Setting up an account overview

Registering is basic but to be considered a Zaarly service expert, you will need to be thoroughly screened and tested on the service that you intend to sell.

Monthly seller fees

1. No registration fees
2. Commission fee of 10%

Possible income levels

The most hardworking service providers of Zaarly report income at around $5000 per month.

Time Requirement
Pros & Cons

Pros

1. Strong support from the platform with feedback and blogs to promote your services
2. Allows an entire team to work on the service.
3. More interactive and friendly to use for customers

Cons

1. Stringent registration as a service provider
2. Limited area of reach.
3. Feedback driven, difficult

Examples

Floor installation
Plumbing services
House cleaning

A getting started Checklist

1. Storefront
2. Prepare to be interviewed and tested
3. Provide references
4. Send an email to apply to be a service provider
5. Payment options

FAQ

When you receive a visit from Zaarly make it the best appointment as possible. Prepare in advance and provide them with a unique customer value proposition that can differentiate you with others in your service category. The more impressed they are with your services, the better are your chances to be awarded as a service expert.

Freelancer

What can be sold?

1. Website development
2. Design, media and architecture
3. SEO marketing
4. Mobile apps
5. Writing and content
6. Data entry and administrative tasks
7. Engineering and science
8. Product sourcing and manufacturing

9. Sales and marketing
10. Business, accounting, human resources and legal
11. Translation and languages
12. Local jobs and trades
13. Other niche services

Setting up an account overview

This platform requires advanced registration. Provide an email address and password. From there, select up to 20 skills that match your expertise. Verify a payment method and upload photos to complete your profile.

Monthly seller fees

1. No registration fees
2. Paid memberships from $0.99 to $199.95
3. Commission fee of 3% to 10%
4. Optional fees from $5 to $199 for additional features

Possible income levels

Contracts range from $35 to $1000 depending on the type of work and expected involvement.

Time Requirement

Like with other freelancing jobs, time is flexible. You can use your entire day to finish a contract quick so you can move on to the next job. Typical contract duration is one week.

Pros & Cons

Pros

1. No withdrawal fees
2. Wide range of services being requested
3. Chat feature

Cons

1. Arbitration fee of 5% or $5 for disputes
2. Tests, required to bid, are paid in advance
3. Bid system may reduce your income

Examples

Data entry
Website mockup
Business cards

A getting started Checklist

1. Portfolio
2. Profile picture
3. PayPal account

FAQ

If you are a beginner, considering bidding low on the projects. Most clients prefer experienced freelancers, who has already done several contracts and received positive feedback. Adjust your bidding rates down the road when you have already built a solid reputation for yourself.

Chapter 4: Specific or Niche Services & Platforms

Surveys Using Globaltestmarket & Crowdology

What can be sold?

Answering surveys is the service for this platform. Online surveys are being done by several companies for different purposes, such as market, academic and other varieties of research. Globaltestmarket and Crowdology receive survey quotas from their clients, which they in turn forward to their members for answering.

Setting up an account overview

These platforms only require basic registration. Provide your first and last name, gender and email address. You have to be at least 14 to 18 years old and a citizen of one of the 49 countries.

Monthly seller fees

No registration fees.

Possible income levels

Due to the relatively minimal effort or input on this service, income is relatively small. Globaltestmarket will pay you with Market Points, which are convertible to cash. For every 1000 points you earn $50. Each survey rewards you within 35 to 250 points. You can acquire these points within a 5 to 6 month period. Crowdology offers you with an immediate payment in cash from $0.40 to $10

Time Requirement

Each survey can be completed within 30 minutes. However, the faster you complete a survey, the more you can take.

Pros & Cons

Pros

1. Easy to do and complete
2. Requires minimal time
3. Earn from referring others to register

Cons

1. Inefficient screening procedure
2. Relatively low income potential
3. Suffers from credibility issues

Examples

Surveys are sent to member emails only. The topics range from automotive, media, social, electronics, tourism, food dining and restaurant and leisure and personal subjects and researches.

A getting started Checklist

No special requirements needed.

FAQ & Best Practices

Read the fine print on the offers of the platform. Make sure that you know what they will pay you in the end, for example if you prefer cash, check that the reward from the task is in the form of PayPal credits since these platforms also use gift cards as payments.

Affiliate marketing Using Amazon Associates & Personal Blogs

What can be sold?

Marketing referral is sold. If you have a personal blog or website and you allow companies to advertise on your website, then you will receive an advertising fee for every successful referral. Success is counted when a visitor, clicks the link on your blog then purchases an item.

Setting up an account overview

Having an Amazon account will automatically allow you to join the Associates Program. On your Amazon profile page, click Join Associates.

Monthly seller fees

No registration fees.

Possible income levels

Commission fees vary depending on the product that you advertise on your blog or site. Range is from 1% such as video game products, to 4% such as grocery, electronic and DVD products to as much as 15% for other specific products.

Time Requirement

Aside from the actual time needed to build and update a blog and upload the links to the Amazon product, virtually no time is required for affiliate marketing.

Pros & Cons

Pros

1. No monetary investment
2. Automatic generation of income without significant input
3. Minimal need for marketing skills

Cons

1. High competition
2. Requires a well-received blog
3. Requires actual purchase

Examples

Kitchen blog
Coffee machines
Fitness equipment

A getting started Checklist

1. A blog or website
2. Amazon account with associates program active

FAQ

Match your blog with the appropriate Amazon product in the market. For example, if you are primarily a technology blog, consider the electronic department of Amazon in your affiliate program. Also make use of the affiliate tools to monitor the number of hits made so you can adjust your advertisements.

Pay per Click Using Swagbucks

What can be sold?

Completing tasks such as watching videos, answering surveys or even playing games are the services that you can provide for this platform.

Setting up an account overview

Swagbucks requires basic registration. It will only ask for your email address or a linked Facebook account.

Monthly seller fees

No registration fees

Possible income levels

Pays you through Swagbucks, one unit of Swagbuck is worth $0.01 but can have higher values depending on how you exchange them. You can either redeem them for actual cash credited to your PayPal account or as gift cards for other reseller platform.

Time Requirement

Different tasks require different time requirements; online surveys can usually be completed for up to 10 minutes, watching videos from around at least 5 minutes or doing a search using provided keywords will take seconds. Earnings can reach $50 to $70 per month.

Pros & Cons

Pros

1. No monetary investment
2. Earn money by doing simple tasks that you may already be doing.
3. Mobile app available for better access

Cons

1. Low income levels
2. Requires several tasks completed to gain convertible Swagbucks
3. Maximum limit on certain gift cards

Examples

Watch a video
Play games

A getting started Checklist

1. Swagbucks toolbar installed

FAQ & Best Practices

Again, reading the fine print is necessary to make sure that you earn from this platform. Open the toolbar once a day will already earn you Swagbucks.

Write Reviews & Feedback Using Slicethepie

What can be sold?

You can write reviews for songs provided by these platforms. Online sales thrive not only on the price but also on the feedback generated on the product. To boost sales, sellers pay for objective reviews.

Setting up an account overview

Slicethepie requires advanced registration. You need to provide your name, email address, birthday, gender, music preferences and race.

Monthly seller fees

No registration fees

Possible income levels

Average review payments are at $0.10 to $ 0.20and you can earn as much as $40 per month.

Time Requirement

You need at least 90 seconds worth of time to listen to the song before you can make and submit review.

Pros & Cons

Pros

1. Commission of 10% for every review by your referral
2. Easy to use
3. Very rewarding especially for music fans

Cons

1. Withdrawal fee of $1
2. Time consuming
3. Minimal revenues

Examples

Review basics
Review samples
Positive and negative feedback

A getting started Checklist

1. Working audio system or speakers
2. Knowledge about music genres

FAQ & Best Practices

You can earn more by writing lengthier reviews that written in good grammar and spelling. You can also gain higher ranks with these quality reviews giving you more songs to listen. Try to write the review as soon as you start listening instead of waiting for the song to end.

Crowdfunding Using Kickstarter, Indiegogo & Gofundme

What can be sold?

Campaigning for pledges to fund a project is the service that you can provide in these platforms. Crowdfunding allows thousands of supporters to donate small amounts of money but due to the sheer volume, the amount collected will add up to huge amounts.

Setting up an account overview

Due to the potential for huge amounts of money, these platforms require advanced registration. Aside from name, address, birthday and email address, you need to provide your social security number, bank account, government issued IDs and debit or credit card accounts.

Monthly seller fees

No registration fee. However, the websites will charge 4% to 5% commission rates to the total amount collected.

Possible income levels

For only one campaign, funds generated reached up to $13 million within 2 months. Income is used as capital for the development of product than can be sold at a profit when manufactured. Campaigners are required to provide a token of appreciation, such as a limited edition version of the campaign product, early access or invitation to donors on the process flow of the campaign.

Time Requirement

Developing a campaign concept and detailed budget may take you at most 1 month. You can run the campaign for one to two months.

Pros & Cons

Pros

1. Efficient fundraising process
2. Variety or project categories
3. International reach

Cons

1. Requires absolute transparency
2. Starting a campaign is only available for certain countries
3. Campaign may fail and you can either return the pledges or claim them at a higher commission rate.

Examples

Ballet shoe clips
Art palette
Mountain bike gear

A getting started Checklist

1. A project concept
2. Marketing collaterals, such as photos or videos
3. Creator handbook for reference

FAQ

Consider visiting the Staff Picks section of the platform. Learn about their most successful campaign so you can take inspiration from them when you plan your own.

Conclusion

The use of these online resources will guarantee you an alternative source of income but to maximize its full benefits, you may consider using a combination of these platforms to reach your monthly thousand targets. As profitable as your goods and services may be, these online resources still require your human touch and attention from time to time.

Remember, the key towards gaining financial freedom is not how many online resources you can use or how much money you profit from your e-businesses. The true measure of your financial success is your ability to amass profit while being a good manager of your money at the same time.

With these online resources complementing your regular work or augmenting your other e-businesses at home, financial freedom is not only a fantasy that you can dream of but a reality that you can truly achieve.

Chapter 6

Insert chapter h

www.ingramcontent.com/pod-product-compliance
Lightning Source LLC
Chambersburg PA
CBHW071002180526
45168CB00003B/1258